Hi! I'm Robot Train. I a lot of deliveries to make for a surprise birthday party today.

Can you help me?

PARTY CENTRAL

Code has English but is a little funny looking!

Great! I need you to program instructions that tell me what to do. This is called code.

How do I get to the present?

Press the moveRight button

Then press run

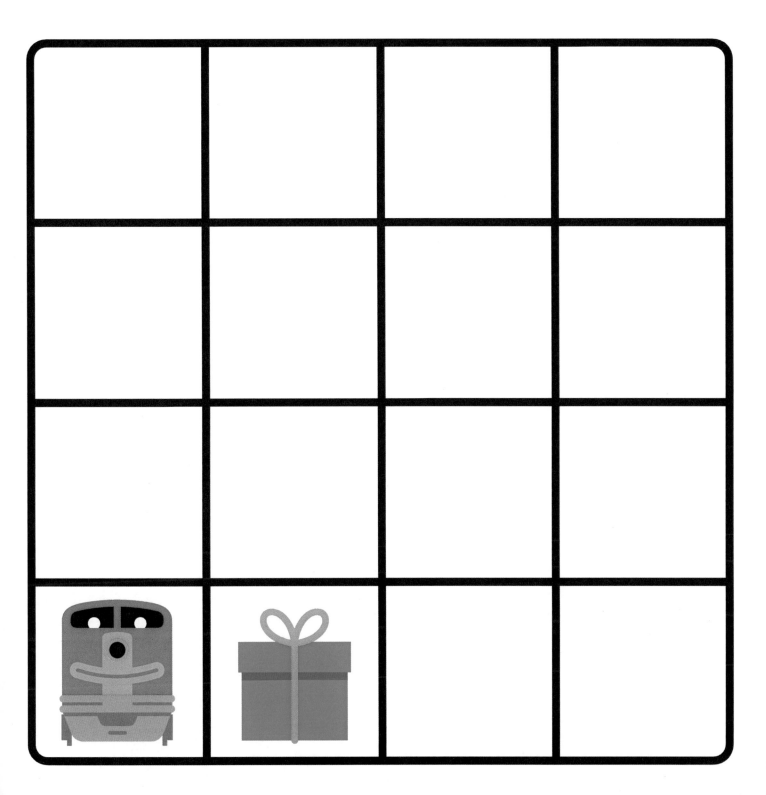

```
moveRight();
```

How do I get to the cupcake?

Press the moveUp button 2 times

Then press run

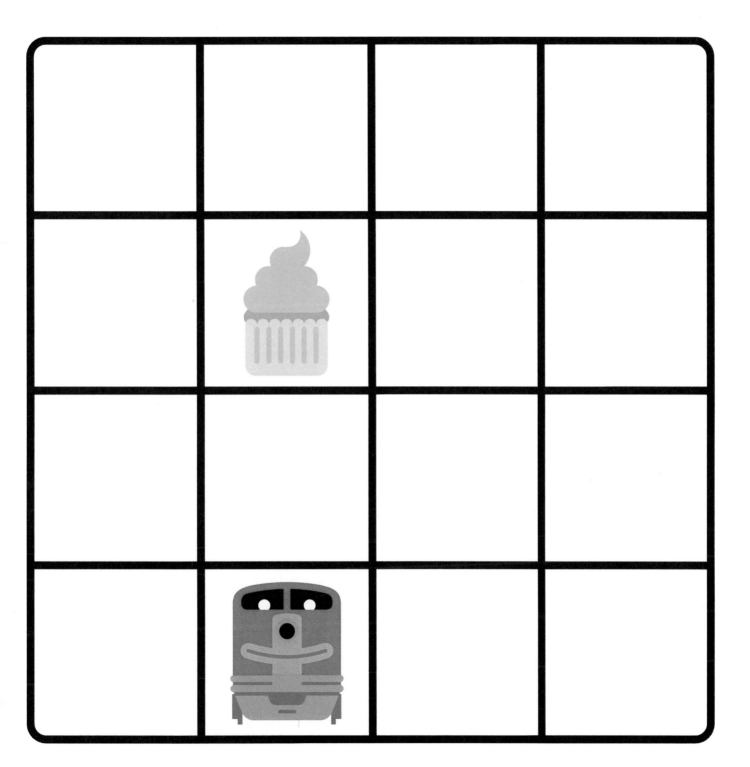

```
moveUp();
moveUp();
```

How do I get to the balloon?

You need 2 arrows: moveLeft and moveDown

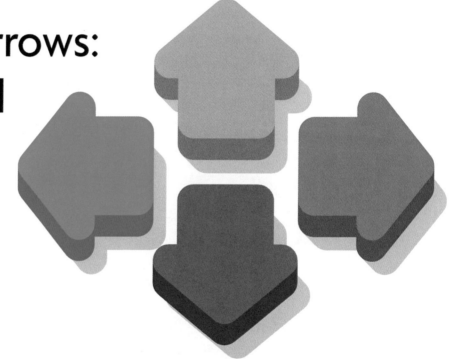

And don't forget to press run

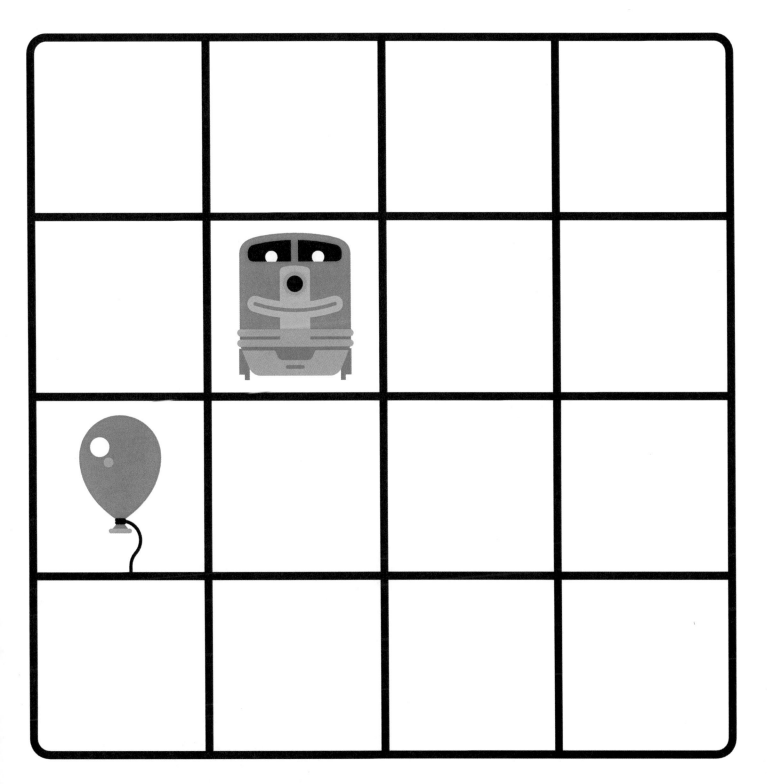

```
moveLeft();
moveDown();
```

Uh oh! There's a bug that's messing up the code!

moveL

Quick! Press the debug button!

That red cupcake looks delicious.

How many times do I need to moveRight?

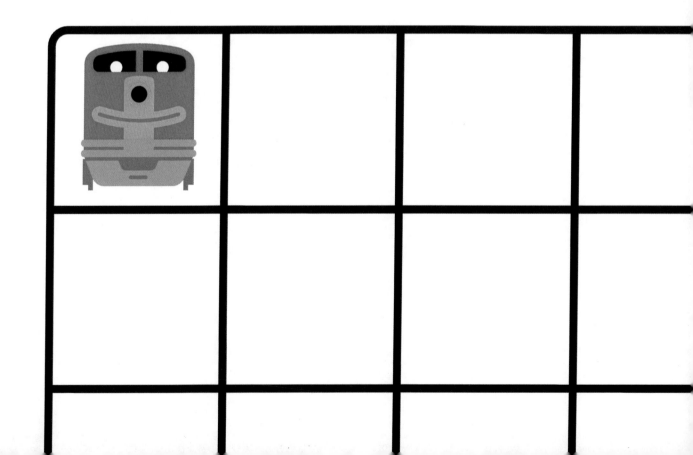

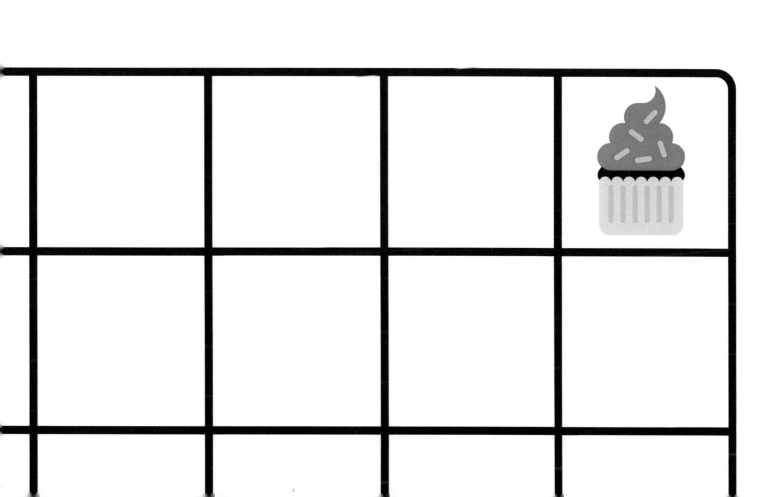

You're right!

Press moveRight
7 times

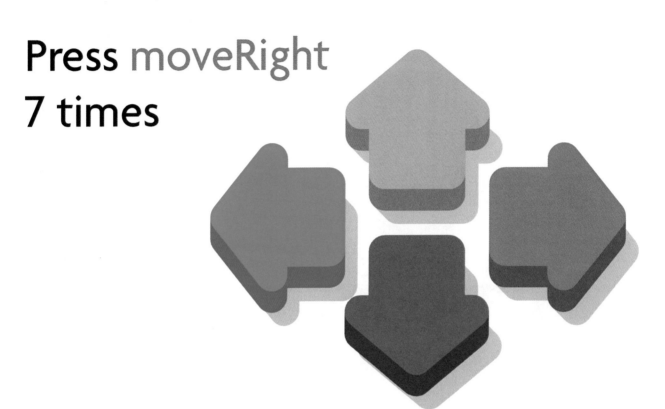

Then press run

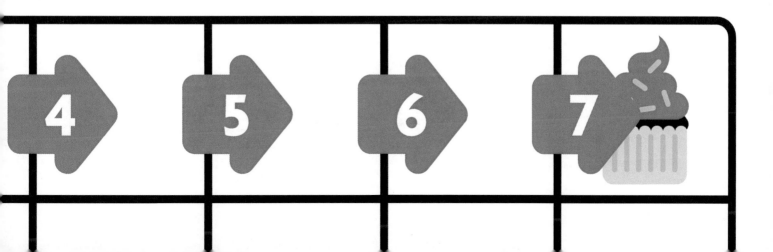

We got it!

It looks so yummy... do you want to take a bite?

You deserve it — you've been writing such awesome code!

Now we just need to get to the party...

Uh oh! There's a fire on the train tracks!

Press the phone to call for help!

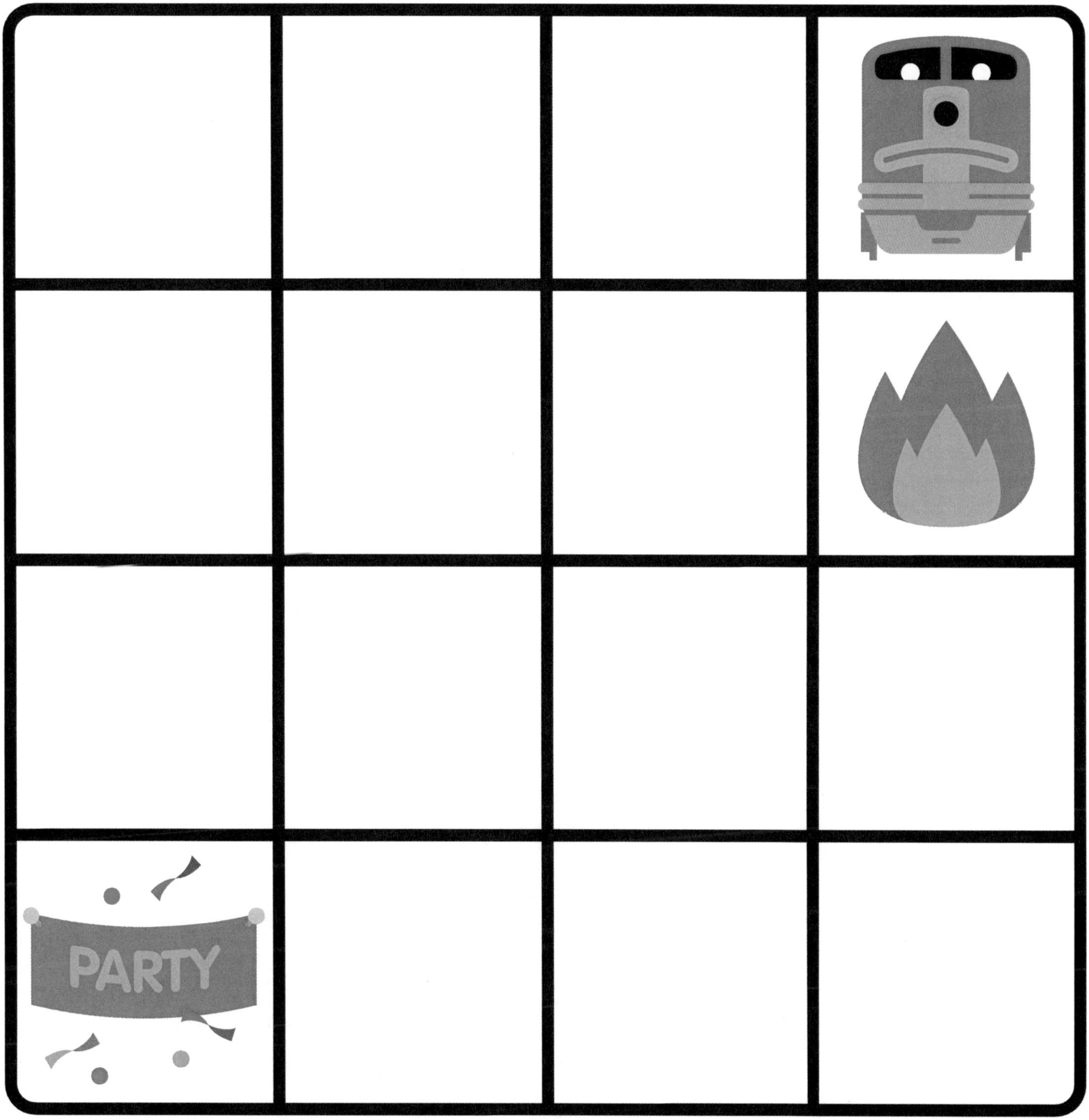
PARTY

Weee woooo weeee woooo!

The fire engine put out
the fire.

Thanks for calling for help!

Code can help me remember to always call for help when I see a fire on the tracks.

IF   THEN

What do I need when it's raining?

IF

THEN

?

An umbrella! Quick – can you put your finger on it and drag it to the right place?

IF   **THEN**

IF   **THEN**

Thanks, super coder!
The cupcakes are safe.

Can you get me to the party?

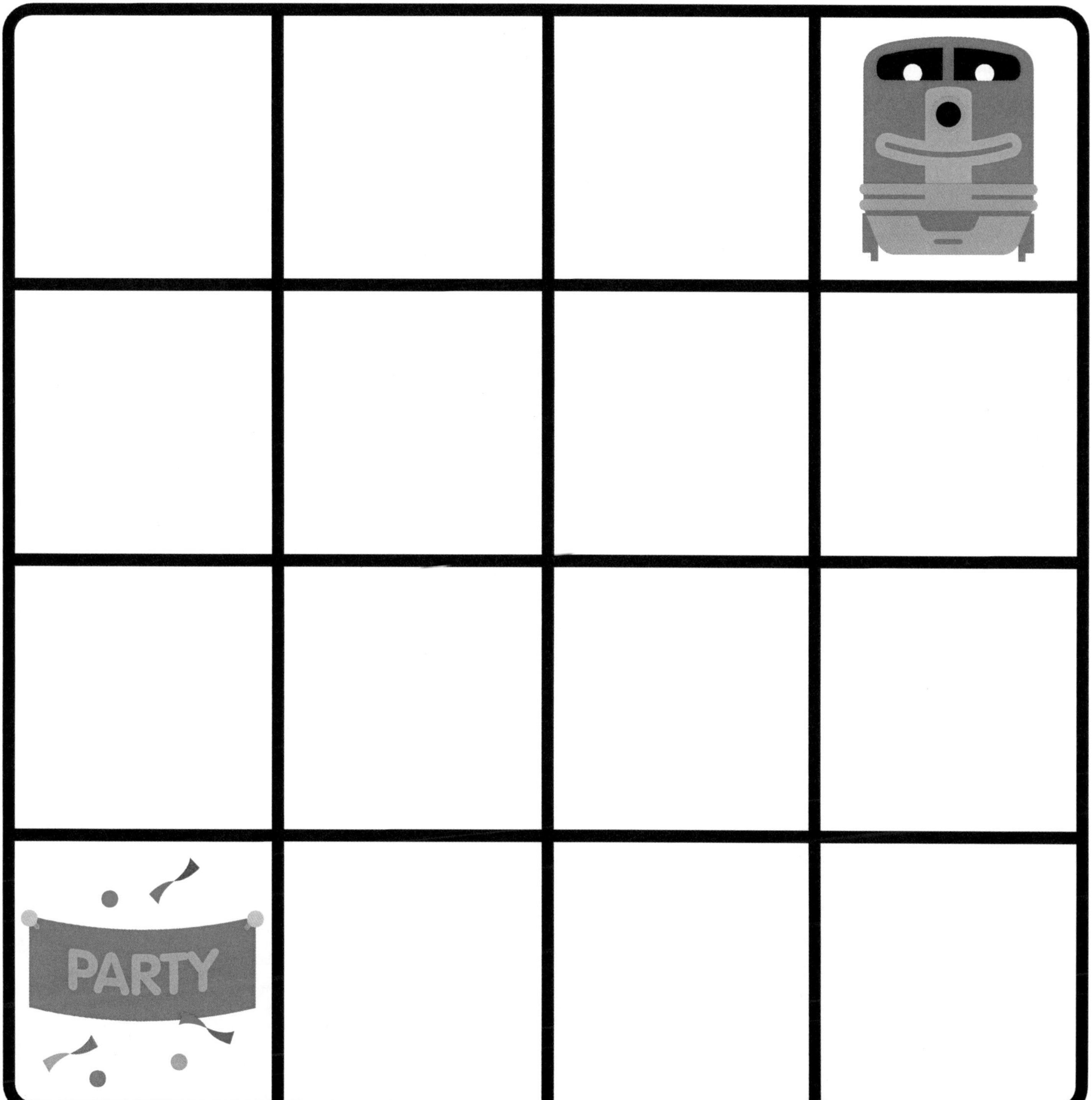
PARTY

We made it!

It's a party for ME?!
Thanks to your code,
it's going to be my best
birthday ever!

Note to parents

Your child and Robot Train covered several important computer programming concepts during their journey to the party:

▶ **Code:** Instructions that can be run by a machine

▶ **Sequence:** Commands must be given in the correct order to work

▶ **Debugging:** Fixing problems in code

▶ **Conditionals:** Something that runs only under certain conditions (If/Then)

The code included is written in JavaScript, the programming language of the web. For more coding practice at home, check out code.org to do online exercises with your child.

If you're interested in bringing coding to your school, contact CodeSpeak Labs at info@codespeaklabs.com.

Activity Pages

How do I get to the balloon?

Write a check mark next to the **arrow** that gets Robot Train going in the correct direction.

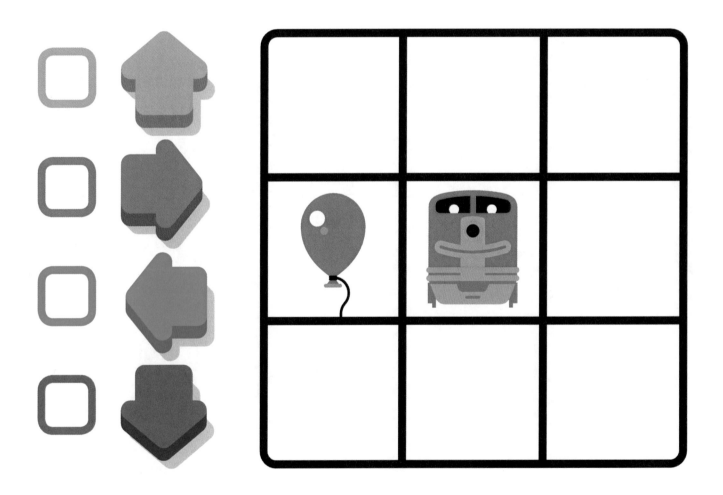

How do I get to the balloon?

Write a check mark next to the **arrow** that gets Robot Train going in the correct direction.

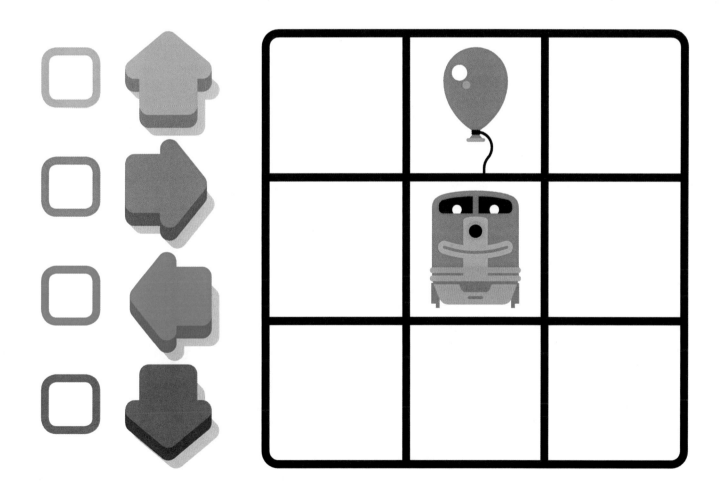

How do I get to the balloon?

*Write a check mark next to the **code** that gets Robot Train going in the correct direction.*

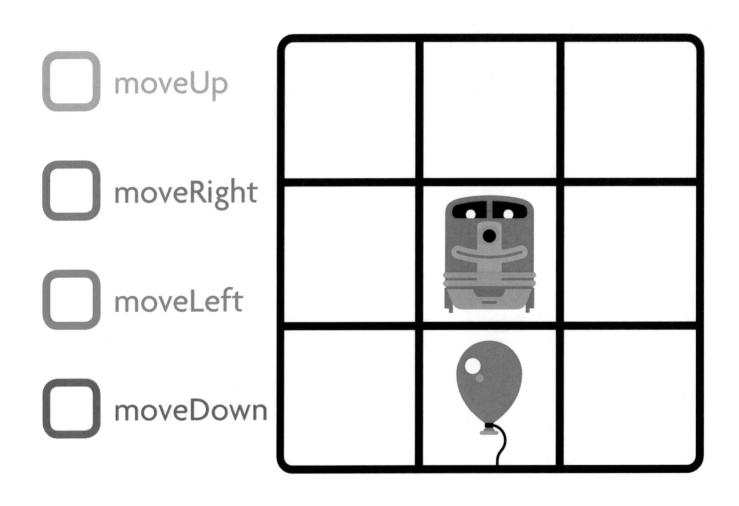

☐ moveUp

☐ moveRight

☐ moveLeft

☐ moveDown

How do I get to the balloon?

*Write a check mark next to the **code** that gets Robot Train going in the correct direction.*

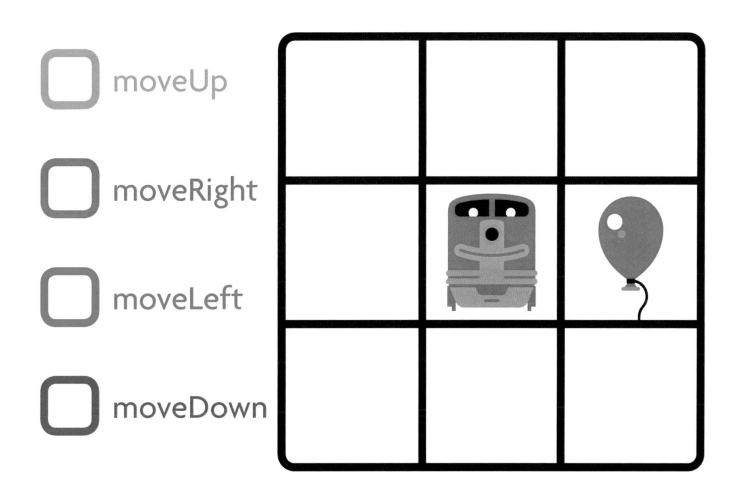

☐ moveUp

☐ moveRight

☐ moveLeft

☐ moveDown

How many times does Robot Train need to moveRight to get to the cupcake?

_____

How many times does Robot Train need to moveRight to get to the cupcake?

_____

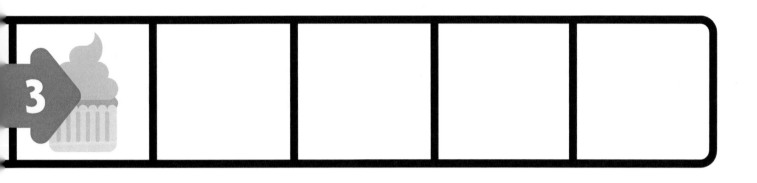

How many times does Robot Train need to moveLeft to get to the cupcake?

_____

How many times does Robot Train need to moveLeft to get to the cupcake?

_____

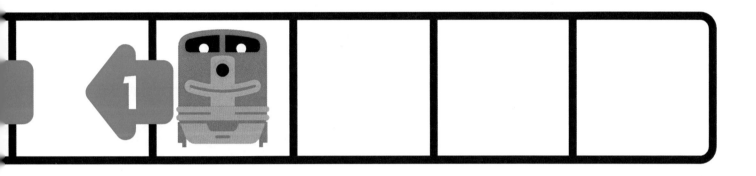

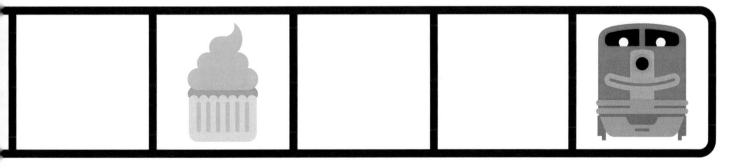

More Fun with Conditionals

You already helped Robot Train with

IF   **THEN**

Help him complete these **IF/THEN** statements. Write a check mark next to the most logical answer.

IF Robot Train is dirty...

THEN he:

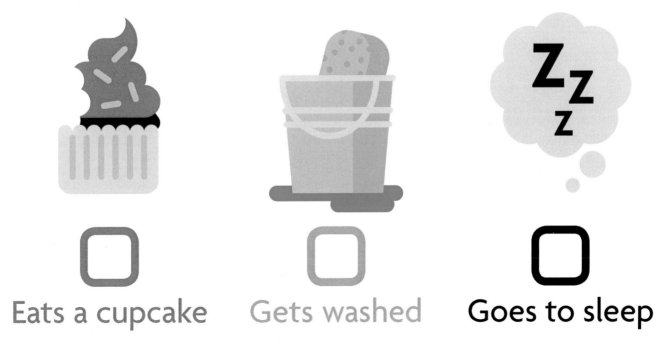

| Eats a cupcake | Gets washed | Goes to sleep |

IF it's bed time...

THEN he:

Eats a cupcake   Gets washed   Goes to sleep

IF Robot Train is hungry...

THEN he:

☐ Eats a cupcake   ☐ Gets washed   ☐ **Goes to sleep**

codebabies.com

Made in the USA
Las Vegas, NV
14 May 2024